Alistair Bryce-Clegg

50

fantastic ideas for
outside all year round

BLOOMSBURY

BLOOMSBURY EDUCATION
Bloomsbury Publishing Plc
50 Bedford Square, London WC1B 3DP, UK
Bloomsbury Publishing Ireland Limited
29 Earlsfort Terrace, Dublin 2, D02 AY28, Ireland

BLOOMSBURY, BLOOMSBURY EDUCATION and the Diana logo are trademarks
of Bloomsbury Publishing Plc

First published in 2015 by Featherstone, an imprint of Bloomsbury Education

Text copyright © Alistair Bryce-Clegg, 2015

Photographs © Fee Bryce-Clegg/ © Shutterstock/ © LEYF

A special thanks to The Friars Primary for their 'Rainbow wind sock' photographs.

Bloomsbury Publishing Plc does not have any control over, or responsibility for, any third-party websites referred to or in this book. All internet addresses given in this book were correct at the time of going to press. The author and publisher regret any inconvenience caused if addresses have changed or sites have ceased to exist, but can accept no responsibility for any such changes

All rights reserved. No part of this publication may be: i) reproduced or transmitted in any form, electronic or mechanical, including photocopying, recording or by means of any information storage or retrieval system without prior permission in writing from the publishers; or ii) used or reproduced in any way for the training, development or operation of artificial intelligence (AI) technologies, including generative AI technologies. The rights holders expressly reserve this publication from the text and data mining exception as per Article 4(3) of the Digital Single Market Directive (EU) 2019/790

A catalogue record for this book is available from the British Library

ISBN: PB 978-1-4729-1342-5; ePDF 978-14729-2475-9

Library of Congress Cataloging-in-Publication Data
A catalogue record for this book is available from the Library of Congress.

10 9 8 7 6

Printed and bound in India by Replika Press Pvt. Ltd

To find out more about our authors and books visit www.bloomsbury.com and sign up for our newsletters.
For product safety related questions contact productsafety@bloomsbury.com

Contents

Introduction 4	Light sabres 35
Wool, wrap wigwam 6	Seed bombing 36
Flower faces 7	Rainbow wind sock 38
Small world stations 8	Water balloon and spoon race 39
Making connections 9	Earth loom 40
Make a water wall 10	Stick sculptures 41
Stinging nettle tea 12	Onion bag birds nest 42
Tree faces 13	Popcorn relay race 44
Tree decorations 14	Ice bowling 45
Paper lampshade decorations 15	Teracotta pot fire 46
Butterfly feeder 16	Shadow faces 47
Collecting stick 17	Shoe organiser garden planter 48
Fairy post 18	Egg splat art 50
Make the own fossils 20	Wind wailers 51
Mud brushes 21	Colour crush 52
Charity shop water play 22	Wall wash 53
Frozen bones 23	Earth worm hotel 54
Make the own dough 24	Puppy obstacle course 56
Biscuit cutter bird treats 26	Captain catch 57
Rock and roll painting 27	Leaf glitter pictures 58
Felt tip rain painting 28	Ice sculptures 59
Tree wrapping 30	Washing line exhibition 60
Mud art 31	Wonderful waterfalls 62
Colour matching game 32	Make a wind streamer 63
Water balloon colour explosion 33	All in knots! 64
Tin can toss 34	

Introduction

Whatever the weather, many young children just love to be outdoors. Indeed, outdoor learning provides children with the potential to learn in a different way – it can be far more physical, faster, louder and bigger!

For many children, playing outdoors may be the only opportunity they have to play safely, assess risk and develop the skills to help them to manage new situations.

The 'ambiguousness' of outdoors also helps children to develop their problem solving and thinking skills, so the more open ended we can keep our outdoor spaces the better.

The Statutory Framework for the Early Years Foundation Stage (2014) expresses the requirement to ensure there is 'access to an outdoor play area or, if that is not possible, ensure that outdoor activities are planned and taken on a daily basis'. In other words, there is an assumption that children will spend at least some of every day outdoors, and that this will apply no matter what the weather brings! However, not all children will have access to the same amount of outdoor space: some settings will have a small patch of grass while others have a field. Nevertheless there are lots of learning opportunities that we can give children that are different from or that build upon the skills and experiences that they have had indoors, no matter how big the available space.

In this book I have collected together some of my favourite outdoor activities, from things that you can make to games that you can play. I have included ideas for all weathers. So, if it's raining, sunny or blowing a gale, there is an idea to get you started! Many of the ideas benefit from the additional space the outdoors environment provides as well as the opportunity to simply try messier activities!

Activity format

All the activities in this series follow the same structure. Starting with 'What you need' which lists the resources required for the activity – the majority are basic resources that are likely to be found already in most settings. It is recommended that you check the 'What you need' list well before embarking on any activity with the children, as well as reading through what the items are needed for. 'Top tip' boxes don't feature in every activity but where appropriate offer a brief suggestion, warning or piece of advice to help in tackling the activity. 'What to do' gives step-by-step instructions for completing the tasks. You should read through the instructions before you start the activity with the children, to ensure you are clear about everything. 'Taking it forward' contains further ideas for additional activities on the same theme. They have been designed to extend the children's experience and broaden their skills. Finally, 'What's in it for the children?' is a brief statement which indicates how the activities contribute to learning.

Outdoor materials and equipment

Some activities involve working with natural materials outdoors. You should remind the children about not putting muddy fingers in their mouths and to wash their hands when they come back indoors. Talk to them about taking care when handling plants and flowers as they may be poisonous.

If activities require the use of tools always make sure an adult supervises the children to avoid accidents. Real tools such as small hammers, screwdrivers, saws, pliers and safe knives are fascinating for young children. Their use can be built into the daily programme provided you explain the risks to children and train them in their safe use.

Food allergy alert

When using food stuffs to enhance the children's play, always be mindful of potential food allergies. Look out for this symbol on the relevant pages.

Skin allergy alert

Some detergents and soaps can cause skin reactions. Be aware of potential skin allergies when letting the children mix anything with their hands. Provide hand-washing facilities for the children to wash materials off afterwards. Watch out for this symbol on the relevant pages.

Safety issues

Social development can only take place when children are given opportunities to experiment and take reasonable risks in a safe environment. Encouraging independence and the use of natural resources inevitably raises some health and safety issues; these are identified where appropriate.

Children need help and good models for washing their hands when using natural materials or preparing food. They may need reminding not to put things in their mouths, and to be careful with real-life or found resources.

Wool wrap wigwam

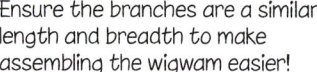

What you need:
- Large sticks/branches
- Coloured wool or twine
- String

Top tip ★
Ensure the branches are a similar length and breadth to make assembling the wigwam easier!

What to do:
1. Take the large sticks and show the children how to wrap sections in coloured wool.
2. When all of the sticks are completely covered, stand them up in a bunch. Let individual children stand in a circle and each hold their sticks, reach above them and gather the ends all together.
3. Loosely bind the ends of the sticks together with string.
4. Let the children spread out the base of their sticks to create a tent/wigwam shaped structure.
5. When you are confident the structure is stable, bind the top of it more securely with the string.
6. Use the wigwam for play, allowing pairs of children to enter inside at a time.

Taking it forward
- Make multiple structures for both indoor and outdoor play. If the structures are well bound at the top then they shouldn't need any further support on the floor.
- Let the children apply the process to small sticks and twigs for their small world play.

What's in it for the children?
The binding of the sticks with the wool is good for children's fine motor dexterity as well as providing opportunities to explore colour and texture. The creation of the structure will allow children to use their construction and negotiation skills, working together.

✚ Health & Safety
Warn the children to be careful they don't catch the sticks or banches in their own eyes or other people's.

Flower faces

What you need:
- Small hand-held mirror
- Petals
- Flowers
- Leaves
- Seeds
- Pieces of A4 paper or card
- Other natural materials
- Digital camera

What to do:
1. Sit together in a large circle and spend some time looking and talking about the children's facial features. Provide a small hand-held mirror and let the children consider their own faces.
2. Talk to the children about key features on their faces, length of hair etc. Avoid any inappropriate comments or rude remarks amongst the children and focus on encouraging positive comments.
3. Next, collect various natural items like flowers and leaves.
4. Help the children to recreate their features using natural materials and to arrange their 'face' on A4 sheets of paper or card.
5. Take a photograph of the finished faces and another of each child.
6. Display copies of the two photographs of each child and compare their likeness!

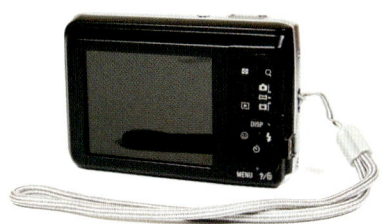

Taking it forward
- You can extend this activity by getting the children to create their whole body or other familiar people or animals.

What's in it for the children?
There will be lots of opportunities for the children to talk about colour and texture and the natural world around them. They will also be developing their knowledge of their own physical features and comparing themselves with each other.

Top tip ⭐
Demonstrate how to use the camera and then let children take turns to photograph their friends and the pictures.

50 fantastic ideas for outside all year round

Small world stations

What you need:

- Tyres of various sizes
- Soil, sand, gravel, pebbles
- Grass seed
- Small plants and shrubs such as dwarf conifer or fern
- Landscaping rocks or pebbles (depending on the size of the tyre)
- Small world figures

What to do:

1. Make sure that the tyres are clean and lay them on a flat surface where the small world play is to take place.
2. Fill each tyre with a different texture: you can plant grass seeds in soil for a 'grassy' area; plant small plants like heather or grasses, set up rocks and pebbles in another tyre.
3. Put the tyres into different areas of the environment to encourage the children to play in different spaces.
4. Introduce different small world figures and encourage the children to use the different terrains for play!

Taking it forward

- Create groups of tyres on different levels for larger small world play spaces.
- Introduce loose items such as sticks, string, pegs and fabric so that children can enhance their play further.
- Use pulleys to connect the small world spaces.

What's in it for the children?

The children will have lots of opportunities to develop their talk and language skills as well as their creativity and thinking skills in the creation of their small world areas.

50 fantastic ideas for outside all year round

Making connections

What you need:
- Plastic waste pipe
- Waste pipe joints
- Junior hack saw

What to do:
1. Cut up the plastic waste pipe into various lengths using the junior hack saw (adult supervised).
2. Add the waste pipe joints to the pre-cut lengths.
3. Let the children experiment with joining the pipes together.

Taking it forward
- You can add the joined piped to an outdoor water play experience and let the children incorporate them into play with small boats.
- Test the pipes with a variety of objects of various sizes to see which will travel down the pipes and which won't.

What's in it for the children?
The children are using their thinking skills to enable them to connect the pipes together. They will also be developing their physical dexterity in trying to move objects down the pipes.

Health & Safety
Only use the hack saw yourself and explain to the children how potentially dangerous it could be.

Making a water wall

What you need:

- Wire mesh, chicken wire or a mesh fence
- Lots of bottles and containers
- Stanley knife (adult only)/ scissors
- Plastic covered wire
- Jugs, funnels and tubing

What to do:

1. Attach the wire or wire mesh to a suitable outdoor wall, fence or frame.
2. Cut two small slits in the back of the bottles or containers and insert a piece of plastic covered wire (this will allow the children to attach the bottle or container to the mesh).
3. Provide the children with a selection of containers, along with funnels, tubing and lengths of plastic coated wire.
4. Let them fill the containers with water and use the funnels and tubing to experiment.
5. The children can attach their filled containers to the mesh to make a water wall.

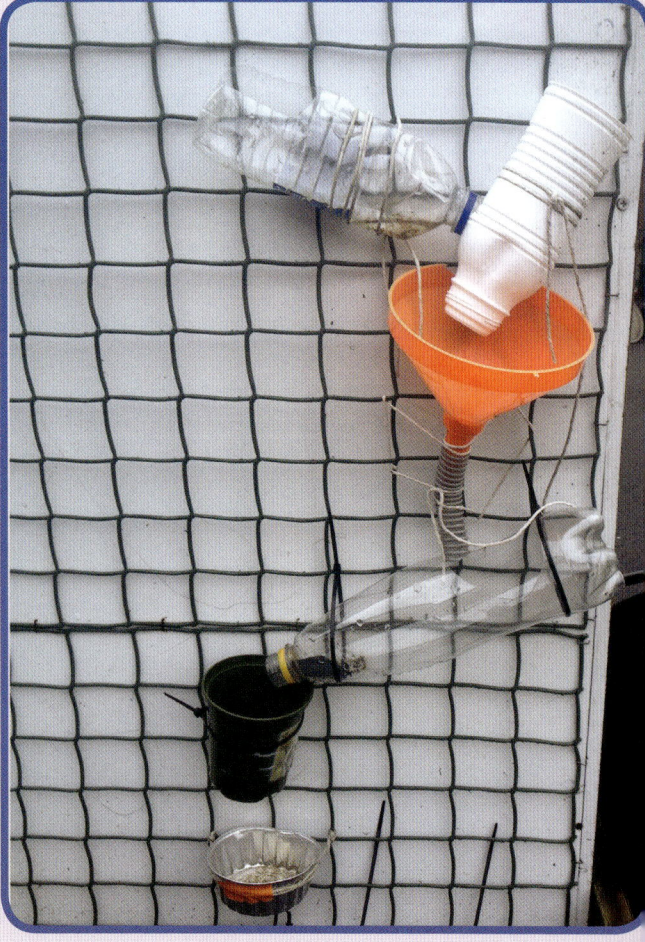

Top tip ⭐

Water play is always a potentially messy activity so make sure the children are wearing suitable clothing and have towels on hand.

50 fantastic ideas for outside all year round

Taking it forward

- You can make these walls on a large and small scale depending on the space you have available.

- Fix some of the resources permanently to the wall to provide the children with a starting structure.

What's in it for the children?

The children will be experiencing the different ways in which water moves as well as using their thinking and problem solving skills to build their wall.

Health & Safety

Make sure an adult cuts the slits in the containers and warn children to take care if the edges are left sharp. Even though the wire is plastic coated, warn the children to be careful not to poke the ends near each other other's faces.

Stinging nettle tea

What you need:

- **Rubber gloves** (for nettle picking)
- **12 fresh stinging nettle leaves**
- **Boiling water**
- **Tea pot**
- **Tea strainer**
- **Sugar** (if required)
- **Small tea cups or beakers**

What to do:

1. Wear rubber gloves to pick the nettles.
2. Put the leaves into the pot and add boiling water.
3. Leave to infuse for three or four minutes
4. Pour through a strainer into a cup, allow to cool a little and invite the children to sample the tea!
5. Ask the children to describe the flavour of the tea and add a little sugar if required.
6. Talk about how you use nettles to make the tea and see if the children know about other plants that are edible.
7. Leave some for the fairies!

Taking it forward

- You can get the children to sample other fruit teas and see if they can identify which fruits are in them. Make a variety of other fruit teas by adding fruit to water and allowing to infuse. Use a cafetière to stop bits of fruit from floating in the tea or let the children experiment with different sizes of sieve to see which works best.

What's in it for the children?

The children have the opportunity to investigate the properties of wild plants.

 Health & Safety
Be aware of any food intolerances and allergies before allowing children to sample the tea.

Tree faces

What you need:
- Mirrors
- Clay or play dough
- Flat surface to roll the dough out
- Selection of natural materials
- Trees or walls to work on

What to do:
1. Start by passing the mirror around and allowing the children to look at their own faces.
2. Next ask the children to each work a piece of clay or dough into a ball about the size of a tennis ball.
3. Show them how to flatten the ball between the hands until it becomes a rough circle.
4. Now press the circle into the bark of a tree or wall.
5. Ask the children to use natural materials to decorate the dough to make a representation of their face. Leave the faces on the trees to welcome the fairies!

Taking it forward
- Use scented dough. Or add some texture to the dough like sand, soil or coffee grounds. It will help the dough to stick a little better.
- If you leave the tree faces out over night, be aware that the slugs might have a munch on them as they seem very partial to a bit of dough!

What's in it for the children?
The children have the opportunity to name all of their facial features. They will be developing the skill of transference and representation as they select natural objects to mimic their features.

Tree decorations

What you need:
- Play dough (various colours)
- Biscuit cutters (various shapes)
- Sequins, glitter, beads
- Natural materials
- Pencil
- Strips of coloured fabric
- Oven if required
- Strips of fabric

What to do:
1. Invite each child to choose a colour of play dough.
2. Roll the dough out to around 2cm thick.
3. Use a cutter to create an interesting shape
4. Allow the children to choose decorative items such as sequins and beads and to push them into their dough shape.
5. Use the pencil to make a hole in the top of the decoration (this is to hang it from the tree).
6. Leave the decorations to air dry or bake in the oven on its lowest heat until hard.
7. When dry, thread a strip of fabric through the hole and hang from a tree or bush.

Taking it forward
- As the dough dries it will shrink so you may need to re-stick some of the decorative items with glue. If you want to weather proof them you will need to give them a coat of clear varnish.

What's in it for the children?
There are lots of opportunities for fine motor development in this activity. The children also have to think about some of their everyday objects in a different way.

Top tip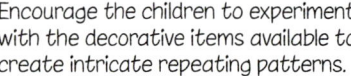
Encourage the children to experiment with the decorative items available to create intricate repeating patterns.

Paper lampshade decorations

What you need:
- Paper lampshades in different sizes
- Paint
- Felt tips
- Collage materials
- Scissors
- Glue
- String, wool or twine

What to do:
1. Assemble your paper lamp shades as per the instructions in the diagrams that come with them.
2. Allow the children to decorate them to their taste!
3. Encourage the children not to use too much glue or paint at once as the paper is fairly delicate and if it gets too wet it will rip.
4. Attach string, wool or twine for hanging purposes.
5. Hang them outside on trees or bushes at any time of the year.

Taking it forward
- Get a number of children to work together on this collaborative project.
- You can add jingle bells to the bottom of the lampshades if you would like them to make a noise in the wind.

What's in it for the children?
The children will have an opportunity to explore a number of aspects of creativity outdoors with lots of mark making possibilities.

Butterfly feeder

What you need:

- Selection of colourful sponges
- String/twine/ribbon/wool
- Pencil
- Nectar (see below)

Nectar recipe

- Four parts boiling water
- One part sugar

Dissolve the sugar in the boiled water to make nectar!

What to do:

1. Talk about some of the wildlife that might visit an outside space.
2. Explain to the children that butterflies can be attracted by sweet things and say you are going to make a butterfly feeder together.
3. Make a hole in each corner of the sponge with a pencil.
4. Thread a length of string, twine, ribbon or wool through each hole and tie.
5. Dip the sponge into the 'nectar'.
6. Tie the sponges up outside to attract the butterflies.

Taking it forward

- Pour the 'nectar' into a wide bowl, bird bath or ceramic plant pot stand and leave it outside a window so the children can watch the butterflies come to drink.
- Plant 'butterfly friendly' plants and shrubs which will also attract butterflies to the setting.

What's in it for the children?

This activity could be an introduction to, or part of learning about the lifecycle of a butterfly. It is also a great opportunity for the children to look at and discuss pattern and colour.

Collecting stick

What you need:
- Sticks approximately 20 cm to 30 cm long
- String, wool, twine or strips of fabric
- Heavy duty tape

What to do:
1. Use tape to attach two of the sticks together to make a 'V' shape (if you can find a 'V' shaped stick that is even better).
2. Show the children how to cover the tape with string, wool, twine or fabric. This will make the handle of the collector.
3. Attach a piece of string, wool, twine or fabric securely to the bottom of one of the sticks (just above the handle).
4. Weave backwards and forwards between the two sticks in a zig zag movement until you get to the top.
5. Secure the string, wool, twine or fabric by tying, or using glue or tape.
6. When you are out looking for natural materials, thread the item you discover in between the strings to keep it in place.

Taking it forward
Have a go at:
- Fill these collecting twigs with seasonal flora and fauna and display them around the setting.
- You can take these sticks with you on nature walks and fill them as you go.
- Create large versions of the same thing, providing you can find a large 'Y' shaped stick.

What's in it for the children?
This is a great activity for fine motor development and also gives the children an unusual way of making their own personal collection of natural things.

Fairy post

What you need:
- Miniature note paper
- Miniature envelopes
- Small pencils

What to do:
1. Explain to the children that they are going to write a letter to the fairies.
2. Allow them to decide what they want to write about.
3. Get the children to record what they want to write or get an adult to write their ideas for them.
4. Ask the children where they think the fairies might collect their post from.
5. Explain to the children that it will have to be a dry place and out of the wind.
6. Identify a suitable spot and leave the letters there for the fairies to collect.

50 fantastic ideas for outside all year round

Taking it forward

Have a go at:

- You could do this as a 'one off' activity or establish a more permanent fairy post box that they children could use on a regular basis.
- If the fairies reply to the children's letters then the children are more likely to write again.

What's in it for the children?

This is a great opportunity to develop mark making skills as well as allowing children to use their imaginations.

The children will also have the opportunity to consider where would be an appropriate place for their postbox so will need to think about weather and waterproofing.

Make your own fossils

What you need:
- One cup used coffee grounds
- Half cup cold coffee
- One and a half cups flour
- Half cup salt
- Mixing bowl
- Wooden spoon
- Suitable 'prehistoric' items

What to do:
1. Explain that you are going to make some special dough together.
2. Measure out all of the ingredients into a bowl.
3. Start with only one cup of the flour and add more if the dough is too sticky to work with.
4. Knead the dough using hands and knuckles, then roll small balls, about the size of the palm.
5. Now, flatten the rounds using the palm of the hand.
6. Press anything that looks interesting into the dough and then remove them carefully.
7. Allow the dough to dry overnight, and you have the very own set of fossils!

Taking it forward
- Replace the coffee grounds with sand or soil for different texture and colour, or add a little of everything until you get the desired consistency.
- You could also embed some real objects into the fossil for extra effect.

What's in it for the children?
The children have first-hand experience of seeing how materials and their properties can change. There are lots of opportunities for language development through exploration of texture. The children will also be experiencing the skill of creating an imprint.

Mud brushes

What you need:
- Twigs and stick
- Grass, leaves, natural materials
- String or strong tape
- Mud!

What to do:
1. Make sure the twig is smooth and has no jagged bits or splinters.
2. Cut the twigs to between 20 and 30 cm.
3. Attach the natural materials to the end of the twigs. You could use more grass to do this (although that can be tricky), string, elastic bands or strong tape.
4. Use different amounts of grass, leaves etc on each twig to create different panting effects.
5. Dip into some mud and paint!

Taking it forward
- You can create these on a huge scale using branches and large leaves such as conifer.
- You can mix powder paint or ready-mixed paint into the mud to create different mud colours.

What's in it for the children?
The children will be exploring a familiar skill (painting) in a less familiar way. They will also experience the textures of the natural materials that they use and also their scent as they cut them and bend them to attach them to their twig.

Charity shop water play

What you need:
- Access to water
- Tin bath (optional)
- If you have not got a tin bath, you can use a water tray or washing-up bowl
- Charity shop or car boot 'pouring resources' like kettles, teapots, milk jugs etc

What to do:
1. Fill up the tin bath or water tray with water.
2. Allow the children to experiment with how the different resources pour.
3. Encourage them to fill and empty using the resources available.

Taking it forward
- Add other resources such as plastic funnels, tubing, syringes and turkey basters to enhance the children's pouring experience.
- Ask the children if they can use more than one resource to pour through and with.

What's in it for the children?
Charity shop finds can be far more engaging than plastic bottles and jugs for lots of children. Because the tin bath or water tray is on the floor, the children get to experiment with pouring from different heights. The metal bath and metal resources also make different sounds as the children pour.

Frozen bones

What you need:
- Plastic bones or miniature dinosaurs
- Large plastic containers (such as ice-cream tubs)
- Natural objects such as fir cones
- Brushes
- Dough utensils
- Safety glasses
- Rubber mallets
- Salt
- Magnifying glasses

What to do:
1. Freeze the bones/dinosaurs in the containers.
2. Add natural objects to the tubs before freezing for a bit more authenticity.
3. Bury the ice blocks in the ground or leave outside for discovery.
4. Allow the children to dig the bones out of the ice using the utensils you have provided.
5. Let the children add the salt to see its impact on the ice and speed up the melting process.
6. If you are using rubber mallets or hammers to chip away at the ice, make sure that the children are wearing safety glasses.

What's in it for the children?
This is an activity full of experimentation and discovery. There is lots to discuss and question. Everyday items can look very different when encased in ice so it is worth spending some time with the magnifying glasses to see what you can find.

Top tip
You could also try adding other things to the ice blocks such as leaf skeletons or moss.

Make your own dough

What you need:

- Two dry food or cereal dispensers
- Flour
- Salt
- **Jugs** (various sizes)
- **Bowls** (various sizes)
- Spoons
- Plenty of water
- Natural materials such as flower petals, sticks, feathers, stones

What to do:

1. Fill one cereal dispenser with salt and the other with flour.
2. Put a small bowl underneath the dispenser that is full of flour.
3. Fill a bowl with two turns of the handle of the cereal dispenser of flour.
4. Put the same bowl under the cereal dispenser of salt.
5. Add one turn of the handle of the cereal dispenser of salt.
6. Slowly add water to the bowl of flour and salt until the dough comes together.
7. If the dough is too wet add more flour.
8. If the dough is too dry add more water.
9. Use the dough to model with.
10. The children can enhance their models by decorating them with natural objects.

Taking it forward

- If you haven't got a cereal dispenser then use bowls of flour and salt and measure with cups.
- You can use a jug of water or provide water in a pump dispenser or a camping reservoir with a tap.

What's in it for the children?

The children are learning about how substances can change when they are mixed together, measuring and capacity – and as you are outdoors, they can make as much mess as they like!

They are also exploring aspects of transient art, modelling and sculpture.

50 fantastic ideas for outside all year round

Biscuit cutter bird treats

What you need:
- Bowl
- Spoon
- Three quarters of a cup of birdseed
- A quarter of a cup of water
- One small packet of gelatin
- String
- Biscuit cutters
- Wax paper
- Skewer

What to do:
1. Talk about how wildlife has little food in the winter and how we sometimes feed the garden birds.
2. Explain you are going to make some tasty treats for the birds.
3. Mix all of the ingredients together in the bowl.
4. Press the mixture into the biscuit cutters.
5. Push the skewer into the bird seed mix inside the biscuit cutter to create a threading hole.
6. Leave to set.
7. Once set, thread some string though the hole and hang outside for the birds to enjoy!

Taking it forward
- Create larger versions of the bird treats as a group activity.
- You can also create a bird hide in the outdoor area using a clothes horse (or similar structure) some old sheets and a camouflage net. Make sure you leave a hole to poke the binoculars through!

What's in it for the children?
The children will be following a recipe and also seeing how the gelatine changes from a liquid into a solid and helps to set the seeds in place.

Once the treats are hanging outside, the children will have a chance to watch the birds that come to eat the treats!

Top tip
Depending on the weather this activity can be done outdoors from start to finish. Or you can create the bird treats indoors and then take them outside to hang.

Rock and roll painting

What you need:
- Large piece of white paper (such as wallpaper)
- Newspaper or cardboard
- Table
- Masking tape
- Paint
- Selection of rocks
- Small bowls/containers

What to do:
1. Attach one end of the paper to the edge of the table with masking tape.
2. Attach the other end of the paper to the ground giving it a gentle slope.
3. Place the newspaper or card at the bottom of the slope (to catch the rocks).
4. Fill each of the bowls with paint and place them on the table at the edge of the paper.
5. The children dip a rock into one colour and roll it down the paper.
6. They can then retrieve their rock and dip and roll again.

Taking it forward
- If you want to do this activity with a larger group of children or with bigger rocks then you might want to put a piece of card between the table and the ground for the paper to rest on.

What's in it for the children?
The children are experimenting with colour and colour mixing as well as exploring creativity, not to mention friction and gravity!

The children will also have the opportunity to talk about how to keep their fingers and toes safe while rolling rocks!

Felt tip rain painting

What you need:
- Washable felt tip pens
- Paper
- Tray or clipboard
- A rainy day!
- Coats and hoods

What to do:
1. Invite the children to each draw a picture, design or pattern onto their paper using the washable markers.
2. Lay their pictures in the bottom of the trays or on the clipboards.
3. When you next have a rainy day, let the children put their coats and hoods on and go out into the rain.
4. The falling rain will change their pictures.
5. Once they are happy with the results tell the children to come back inside.
6. Leave their papers to dry in a warm spot and have a look together at the changes that have happened. Can they describe their pictures now?

Taking it forward

- Depending on the size of tray that you have available, you can do this activity using various sizes of paper.
- Use a builder's tray and some lining paper for a really large version of this activity.

What's in it for the children?

The children will have the opportunity to apply their own creative skills to their pictures. They will also be experiencing cause and effect and changing substances as the rain alters the pictures that they have made.

Top tip

Make sure the colours from the pens don't run onto clothing. Show the children how to hold their pictures away from them in the rain.

Tree wrapping

What you need:
- Different types of fabric
- Coloured paper (e.g. crêpe)
- Ribbon
- Tape
- Safety pins

What to do:
1. Encourage the children to sort through the fabrics and to cut the fabric and paper into strips of different lengths.
2. Demontrate how to wrap the lengths of fabric and paper around the trunk and branches of the tree.
3. Secure with tape or safety pins.
4. Tie the ribbon around the trunk or branch of the tree allowing it to blow and trail in the wind.

Taking it forward
- This can be done on both a large and small scale. Tree wrapping is great for short periods of time, but should not be left on trees permanently as it can cause damage to the bark.
- You can add jingle bells to the ends of the ribbons and streamers to make them 'jingle' in the wind.

What's in it for the children?
The children will be using both gross and fine motor dexterity when decorating their tree. They will also have to think about methods of joining.

Top tip
Invite the children to bring in a selection of unwanted fabric pieces or garments that can be cut up, from home.

Mud art

What you need:

- **Mud** (garden mud, not compost: you can purchase sterilised top soil if you haven't got access to the own)
- **Powder paint or liquid water colour**
- **Containers or various sizes**
- **Water**
- **Washing-up liquid**
- **Spoons or other stirring implements**
- **Large and small paintbrushes** – you could also use washing-up brushes and pan scrubs for a different effect
- **Measuring cups**

What to do:

1. Take a cup full of mud.
2. Start with three tablespoons of powder paint, you can always add more.
3. Add a squirt of washing-up liquid (optional).
4. Slowly add water and stir.
5. Paint with the mud paints.

Taking it forward

- You can use mud to paint on paper or direct onto other outdoor surfaces such as paving stones, bricks and tree trunks.
- Add other materials to the mud to add texture.

What's in it for the children?

The children are having the opportunity to explore the familiar skill of paint mixing in an outdoor environment. They will also be experiencing lots of smells and textures.

Colour matching game

What you need:

- Chalk of varying colours and sizes
- Paint colour charts (optional)
- Natural objects such as flowers, leaves

What to do:

1. Use chalk to create a number of small rectangles of colour on the ground.
2. If you are working with group of children, put the rectangles in different places to make them easy to access.
3. You can group the chalk rectangles by shade or have a multi-coloured mix.
4. Ask the children to hunt for objects such as flowers and leaves etc that match the chalk colours.
5. Talk to the children about what they are allowed to pick or collect.

Taking it forward

- Add a colour paint chart to the chalk rectangle for an extra level of challenge.
- Use a digital camera to take pictures of the collections and display.

What's in it for the children?

The children are using their looking, matching and grouping skills to collect objects that match the chalk rectangles.

Water balloon colour explosion

What you need:
- Water balloons
- Plastic bowls
- Ready-mixed paint
- Paper
- Bowl of soapy water (optional)

What to do:
1. Fill the water balloons (carefully) and tie them at the top. The children will enjoy filling the balloons, but will struggle to tie them so make sure that there is an accomplished balloon tier on hand!
2. Hold the balloon by the knot and dip it into paint.
3. You can either dip the end of the balloon or the whole balloon.
4. Print or roll the balloon onto the paper.
5. Repeat the process until the paper is full.
6. Make repeating patterns or images.

Taking it forward
Once you have completed the outdoor work, drop the balloons onto the painting and see how it changes once the balloons burst.

What's in it for the children?
The children are exploring the skill of printing as well as experiencing texture and movement.

Top tip
You might want to wash the balloons in between dips - unless you want lots of murky brown pictures!

Tin can toss

What you need:
- Two large 'Y' shaped sticks
- One long straight stick
- Tape
- String
- Tin cans of different sizes
- Small ball

What to do:
1. Push the two Y shaped sticks into the ground and lay the straight stick across them.
2. Attach string to the tin cans using tape.
3. Loop the cans over the straight stick.
4. Children should stand at a reasonable distance away from the structure.
5. The children can throw the ball and try and get it into the can.

Taking it forward
- You can always add a number score to each of the cans to turn this activity into an adding game.
- Give the children a variety of different sized and shaped balls to add more challenge.

What's in it for the children?
Children will be working on their gross motor and hand-eye coordination skills as well as learning how to take turns.

Light sabres

What you need:
- Cardboard tubes
- Felt tips in a variety of colours
- Stickers, sequins etc
- **Balloons** (long sausage shaped ones)

What to do:
1. Make the own light sabres from a cardboard tube and a balloon!
2. Take a cardboard tube and decorate it with felt tips, stickers, sequins etc.
3. Put a balloon inside the tube.
4. Slowly blow up the balloon keeping the tube near the mouth (this keeps the tube tight on the balloon).
5. Once fully inflated, tie the balloon and you are ready for battle.
6. Encourage the children to have fun with the light sabres but ensure safety at all times when playing with balloons.

Taking it forward
On a hot day, replace the cardboard tube with some grey pipe insulation and the balloon with an ice-pop.

What's in it for the children?
Alongside their creativity skills when creating their light sabres, the children will be enhancing their gross motor development as they use them.

Top tip
You could always cover the tubes in paper first or decorate the paper and glue it to the tube if that's easier.

Seed bombing

What you need:
- Two cups of flour
- Bowl
- One cup of compost
- One cup of water
- Two packets of wild flower seeds
- Baking parchment
- Mixing spoon

What to do:
1. First add the flour to the bowl, then add the compost, next add the water and finally add the seeds.
2. If the mixture is too wet add more compost. If it is too dry and crumbly, add more water.
3. Pull off small pieces of the 'dough' and roll into balls between the palms of the hands.
4. Lay the compost/seed balls onto a sheet of baking parchment.
5. Leave to dry out (usually about two days depending on the size of the balls).
6. Take the seed bombs and throw around the outdoor space.
7. Wait for the seeds to grow!

Top tip
Try and pick spaces where there is little or no growth so you will know that it has worked.

Taking it forward

- If you don't want to just throw the seed bombs, you can also use a catapult to fire them into the shrubbery!
- If it is really dry when you seed bomb, it might be worth giving the ground a squirt with a hose first.

What's in it for the children?

The children will be learning lots about how plants germinate and what seeds need to help them to grow. Unless you have used cress seeds, they will also need to develop patience!

Rainbow wind sock

What you need:
- **Tin cans**, (any size)
- **Primer**
- **Paint** (in rainbow colours)
- **Glue gun and glue stick**
- **Ribbon**
- **Nail and hammer or drill**
- **String**

What to do:
1. Tell the children you are going to male a wind sock to measure the wind direction.
2. Work with the children and let them help to make the sock.
3. Paint the tin can with the primer, one coat is usually enough and you will only need to paint the outside of the tin.
4. Use the glue gun to stick various ribbons and streamers to the open end of the tin can.
5. Hammer a nail into the solid end of the can to create a hole and thread the string through the hole.
6. Knot the string inside the can to stop it from slipping through.
7. Hang the finished rainbow wind sock somewhere where the wind will blow it and note which direction the streamers flow to show the wind direction.

Taking it forward
- You can make multiple cans in multiple sizes to hang outside.
- Add bells to the end of the ribbons and streamers.
- Laminate photographs of the children and add those to the streamers.

What's in it for the children?
Alongside developing their creative skills, the children will be learning about weather and the effect that wind can have on objects.

Water balloon and spoon race

What you need:
- Water balloons
- Water
- **Wooden spoons** (or a scoop if you want to make it a bit easier)
- **Marker** (for the start and finish)

What to do:
1. Fill the water balloons with water and tie.
2. Select a suitable area for you the race and mark out the beginning and end of the chosen race track.
3. Ask four or five children to line up at the start of the race track. Give them each a spoon and place a balloon onto each of the wooden spoons.
4. Start the race. Tell the children they must get to the end with their balloons still in place on the spoon.
5. If the children drop their balloon they need to go back to the start.

Taking it forward
- To make the race harder, you can introduce obstacles. To make it easier, you can create a shorter course or give the children a deeper spoon or scoop.
- You can also combine this idea with the classic three-legged race and tie two children's legs together before they run.

What's in it for the children?
The children will be developing their gross motor skills, hand-eye coordination, balance and speed as well as having some physical exercise.

Earth loom

What you need:
- Four large branches/sticks: two long, two short
- A large amount of string
- A rubber mallet
- Selection of natural materials such as grasses and leaves

What to do:
1. Push the long sticks into the ground just less than the width of the short sticks apart.
2. Attach one of the short sticks to the top of the long sticks (like a picture frame) binding the corners securely with string.
3. Repeat at the bottom with the other short stick.
4. Make sure that the children can reach the frame!
5. Loop the string around the length of the two shorter sticks repeatedly to create a loom.
6. Get the children to thread natural materials such as grass and leaves in between the sticks using it like a loom.

Taking it forward
- You can make large looms with big sticks, but you can also create smaller looms for individual work.
- You could apply the same principle to railing or fencing in your outside space if you haven't got access to large sticks.

What's in it for the children?
Whilst weaving into the loom, the children will be working on their fine and gross motor dexterity. They will also be experiencing the texture of lots of natural materials giving them plenty of opportunity for talk and discussion. They will be able to experience sequence and pattern as well as exploring creativity.

Stick sculptures

What you need:
- Collection of different shaped and sized sticks and logs – depending on the size of sculpture you might need to collect quite a few
- Other natural materials for enhancement (rocks, log slices etc)

What to do:
1. Decide together with the children what you are going to make the sculpture of. It could be a person, an animal or just shapes.
2. Think about how big you want the sculpture and how many sticks you will need.
3. Talk to the children about the key features of the thing that you are going to feature in the sculpture.
4. Start by creating a rough outline with sticks. You can also use string, which is a little easier to handle and move.
5. Fill in the outline with sticks and other natural materials for depth and texture.
6. Stand back and admire the work!

Taking it forward
- Before you start the large scale piece of work you might want the children to experiment with twigs, leaves and stones to create something on a smaller scale first.
- Talk to the children about how you can create pattern and texture by layering sticks and materials on top of each other.

What's in it for the children?
Children will be using some of their higher order thinking skills with this task.

Onion bag birds nest

What you need:

- Mesh onion or fruit bag
- Wool, string, ribbon thread
- Human hair (see Top tip)
- An old bird's nest (if you find one that has been abandoned)

What to do:

1. Talk to the children about what birds need/use to build a nest.
2. Show them a real bird's nest or some pictures of the way different birds build their nests.
3. Ask the children to collect items from indoors and out that they think would be suitable for a bird to use in their nest building.
4. Fill the mesh bags with the collected resources allowing a few bits to poke out through the holes.
5. Tie the bags at the top.
6. Hang the bags in trees or from bird tables and wait for the birds to visit.

Taking it forward

- Provide the children with binoculars so that they can watch the birds collecting their nest building materials.

- Go on a nest hunt and see if you can see any of the things that you collected being used.

What's in it for the children?

The children are thinking about how animals live and what they can do to help them to survive.

Top tip ⭐

Ask the children to collect some of their hair when they have been to the hairdressers. Not only is it good for making nests it is a great talking point.

Popcorn relay race

What you need:
- Clear plastic cups
- Elastic bands
- Paperclips
- Popcorn
- Scissors

What to do:
1. Make a small hole in the bottom of two plastic cups.
2. Push the end of an elastic band up through the hole.
3. Push the paperclip onto the end of the elastic band.
4. Pull the elastic band from underneath the cup until the paperclip is securely across the bottom.
5. Loop the elastic band over a child's shoe with the cup on top.
6. Fill the cups with popcorn.
7. Set up a short race track with a start and a finish.
8. Encourage the children to run the race, trying not to spill any popcorn.

Taking it forward
- Use a timer so that the children have to finish the course in a given time.
- Work in teams and get the children to tip the popcorn that is left in their cups into a bucket. The one with the fullest bucket at the end wins.

What's in it for the children?
The children are really working on their balance and coordination as well as developing team and game playing skills.

Ice bowling

What you need:
- Balloons
- Food colouring (optional)
- Freezer
- Construction kits such as Duplo or Lego

What to do:
1. Fill the balloon with water until it is the size you require and tie.
2. Put the tied balloons into the freezer and freeze for a least eight hours or overnight.
3. Invite the children to make towers of construction bricks, making each tower a different colour.
4. Position the towers together.
5. Take the balloon out of the freezer.
6. Cut the end off the balloon (where the knot is).
7. Peel back the balloon and throw away.
8. You should now have some coloured ice bowling balls.
9. Ask the children to bowl the ice balls and see how many towers they can knock down.

Taking it forward
- You can use large bricks for an easier game or make it harder with smaller construction bricks.
- You could give each coloured tower a numerical score and ask the children to add up their scores as they knock them down.

What's in it for the children?
The children are consolidating their hand-eye coordination, balance and gross motor skills.

The children will also be experiencing the changing state of water as it changes from a liquid into a solid and then back to liquid again.

Top tip
If you are using food colouring, add it before you put in the water.

Terracotta pot fire

What you need:
- Small terracotta plant pot with a hole in the bottom
- A length of tin foil per pot
- **Charcoal** (enough to fill each pot to two thirds)
- **Pot of Vaseline** (a little goes a long way!)
- Cotton wool balls
- Matches or a flint fire stick

What to do:
1. Talk to the children about fire safety and make clear rules about what they can and cannot do and touch around fire.
2. Line the terracotta pot with tin foil.
3. Fill the pot two thirds of the way up with charcoal.
4. Rub a couple of the cotton wool balls in Vaseline.
5. Tuck the balls in between the charcoal.
6. Using the matches or fire stick, light the cotton wool (this will act like a fire lighter).
7. The fire will initially burn with flames and then the charcoal will become white (like a barbeque).
8. The fire pot will stay hot for a long time.

Taking it forward
- You can make larger versions for a group activity.
- Use the terracotta pot fires to toast marshmallows.
- Add twigs and sticks to the fire to keep them burning.

What's in it for the children?
The children can learn about the positive aspects and the danger of fire. They will have lots of opportunities to talk about heat and how it affects the things around it.

Health & Safety
Never leave children unattended near matches or fire. Warn children of the danger of playing with or handling matches.

Shadow faces

What you need:
- Smooth pebbles (small)
- Magazines with pictures showing faces
- PVA glue
- Scissors
- Paintbrush
- Sunny day

What to do:
1. Choose pebbles that are a similar size and shape to eyes, nose and mouth.
2. Ask the children to help you cut out a selection of eyes, noses and mouths from pictures in magazines.
3. Invite them to select appropriate pebbles and, using the PVA, glue the eyes, noses and mouths to the pebbles.
4. Allow to dry, then give an extra couple of coats of PVA for protection.
5. On a sunny day get the children to position the pebbles on the ground to make a face and then stand with their backs to the sun so that the pebbles make the face of their shadow.

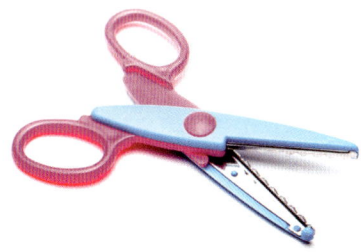

Taking it forward
- Add in extra features like ears or hair.
- Cut out some animal features and get the children to turn themselves into shadow animals.

What's in it for the children?
The children are learning about light and shadow as well as their facial features and how they are placed in relation to each other.

Shoe organiser garden planter

What you need:

- Shoe organiser
- Scissors
- Gravel
- Compost
- Plants or seeds
- Watering can and water

What to do:

1. Put five or six holes in the back of each section of the shoe organiser. This will become the bottom of the planter.
2. Lie the shoe organiser down so that the holes you have created are on the ground and the open space is at the top.
3. Put a small amount of gravel into each section of the shoe organiser for drainage.
4. Fill each section with compost until it is almost full.
5. Sprinkle the seeds or plant the plants.
6. Water well and wait for the plants to grow.

Taking it forward

- If you can find a shoe organiser that has clear plastic sides the children will be able to can see the roots as the plants grow. If you have a fabric shoe organiser, you can always decorate it with permanent marker or fabric paint.

What's in it for the children?

The children will be learning about plants and what they need to survive, as well as doing a bit of recycling.

Top tip

The planter will be heavy and difficult to move once it is finished, so it is best to create it in the space where you would like it to stay. The shoe organiser planter will grow best in a sunny position.

Egg splat art

What you need:
- Lots of eggs
- Teaspoon
- Bowl
- Paint
- Large sheet of paper

What to do:
1. Tap the end of the raw egg with the spoon to crack the shell (this is easier than it sounds).
2. Remove the cracked bit of shell with a spoon (as you would a boiled egg).
3. Pour the egg into you bowl (you can use this for another project).
4. Carefully wash the empty egg shells in hot soapy water.
5. Once dry, fill the egg shells with paint.
6. Throw the paint filled eggs at the paper and create some art.

Taking it forward
- You can throw other things at the paper such as rinsed out tea bags, balls, cotton wool balls or sponges.
- You can collect all of the broken egg shells, rinse them and use them for other projects in the creative area or in an exploratory tray.

What's in it for the children?
The children are creating art as well as working on their gross motor dexterity, balance and coordination.

Health & Safety
Take care with raw egg and warn the children not to eat any of it. Wash hands after handling the eggs.

Wind wailers

What you need:
- **Plastic bottles** (various sizes)
- **Long sticks or wood**
- **Strong tape**
- **Hammer**
- **Scissors or craft knife** (adult only)
- **Permanent marker**

What to do:
1. Turn the bottle upside down. The bottom of the bottle is going to become the top of the head of the wind wailer.
2. Use the scissors or craft knife to cut a vertical section of plastic out of the bottle (adult only).
3. This section can be anything between 8 cm and 20 cm long and 6 to 17 mm wide (different sized sections will make different sounds in the wind).
4. Using the cut section as a nose, ask the children to add other features to the bottle using the permanent marker.
5. Hammer or push the sticks into the ground.
6. Tape the neck of the bottle onto the stick.
7. Wait for the wind to make the bottles 'wail'.

Taking it forward
You could use other resources to decorate the bottles. Just remember that they will be outside in the wind and the rain.

What's in it for the children?
This is an activity that gets children thinking and talking. How does a hole in a bottle make such an unusual sound? Great for early scientific exploration.

Colour crush

What you need:
- Old chalk in a variety of colours
- Wheeled toys such as bicycles, trikes and scooters
- Water or a rainy day
- Spray bottles
- Paper (small pieces for individual projects or lining paper for a group project)

What to do:
1. Break the coloured chalk into small pieces.
2. Scatter the chalk on the ground (fairly close together).
3. Ask the children to ride their wheeled toys over the chalk repeatedly to crush it.
4. Once crushed, ask the children to ride by and squirt the chalk, or if done on a rainy day, just let the rain do its work!
5. When the chalk is wet either lay paper over the top of it and get the children to ride over the paper or ask the children to ride through the wet chalk and then over the paper.
6. Children can ride forwards and then reverse repeatedly until the desired effect is achieved.

Taking it forward
- If you work on individual pieces of paper then you can display these together to create a collage. Larger pieces of paper such as lining paper can be used to produce a collective piece of artwork.

What's in it for the children?
The children are using their gross motor skills as well as experimenting with the transforming of materials, colour mixing and a little bit of creative art work thrown in for good measure.

Wall wash

What you need:

- Chalk (large playground chalk works best)
- Paintbrushes in various sizes
- Emulsion paintbrushes
- Wallpaper brushes
- Dustpan brushes
- Sweeping brushes
- Small squeezy bottles
- Spray bottles

What to do:

1. An adult needs to chalk all over an outside wall in advance (you could blame this on an angry elf or a misbehaving fairy)!
2. The children use the brushes and water bottles to clean the wall.
3. Different brushes can be used to clean different sections of the wall. Hand brushes are good for low down and long handled brushes for the top of the wall.

Taking it forward

- Adults can use this activity to impact on children's gross and fine motor development. Children needing to develop their gross motor skills use the large brushes and children needing fine motor practice, the squeezy bottles.

What's in it for the children?

The children will need to talk and work together as well as developing their physical dexterity. It is hard work to scrub off all of the chalk, so it should give them a good upper body workout!

Earth worm hotel

What you need:

- Large clear plastic bottle
- Smaller plastic bottle
- Pea gravel or aquarium gravel
- **Soil** (not compost)
- Sand
- **A pair of washed tights** (one leg for each earth worm hotel you create)
- Elastic bands
- Some worm guests for the hotel

What to do:

1. Cut the top off the large plastic bottle, about a third of the way down.
2. Keep the bottom and discard the top.
3. Put a small layer of gravel in the bottom of the bottle.
4. Fill the small plastic bottle with water (just to give it some weight).
5. Place the small plastic bottle inside the big one (this will encourage the worms to move around the outside of the worm hotel).
6. Begin to fill the large bottle with alternate layers of soil and sand about 2 cm deep.
7. Once the bottle is half full, add the worms and carry on filling.
8. Cover the top of the jar with a piece of the tights to stop the worms from escaping!
9. Secure the tights with the elastic bands.

Top tip

The best way to collect worms is to soak a piece of ground with buckets of water or a hose and then create vibrations with your feet!

Ask parents to donate unwanted, washed tights for the project.

Taking it forward
- You will need to feed the worms by dropping a small amount of vegetation into the top of the 'hotel'.
- If you cover the outside of the hotel you will be more likely to see worm tunnels.

What's in it for the children?
This is a great activity for developing children's observation skills and interest as well as their understanding of worms and what they do.

Health & Safety
Remind the children that worms are living things and teach them how to handle them carefully.

Puppy obstacle course

What you need:
- Tyres
- Cones
- Ropes
- Toy dogs
- Dog collars
- Dog leads
- Digital timer
- Clip board
- Paper
- Mark making materials
- Cups, trophies, certificates (optional)

What to do:
1. Set out the tyres, cones and ropes (and anything else that you can find) as an obstacle course.
2. Give each toy dog a collar and a lead.
3. Each child takes it in turn to take a dog through all of the obstacles in the obstacle course as a contestant.
4. Another child takes on the role of judge and times how long it takes the dog and their owner to complete the course.
5. The judge records the times on a clipboard.
6. The winner is presented with a certificate or trophy.

Taking it forward
- To make the activity harder, make the course longer or more complex.
- Get the children to use the resources to design their own course.
- Introduce milk crates, bread crates, planks for balancing and lots of other open ended resources to encourage the children's creative thinking.

What's in it for the children?
This activity builds on children's interests in dogs. Encourage them to use their thinking and planning skills for creating a course. It also introduces an element of competition and the challenge of working against a timer.

Captain catch

What you need:
- A group of children
- A ball (about the size of a football)

What to do:
1. Depending on the number of children you have, split them into teams.
2. Each team has a captain who stands about a metre away from their team and faces them.
3. The captain starts with the ball.
4. The captain throws the ball to the first member of the team who throws it back and sits down.
5. The captain repeats this action with all team members.
6. When the last team member catches the ball he runs to replace the captain, everyone stands up, the 'old' captain joins the front of the line and the game starts again.

Taking it forward
- Changing the size of the ball to a smaller ball makes it more challenging. For younger players you can use a balloon, but the captain needs to stand a lot closer to his team.
- The first time the children play the game, an adult can take on the role of the Captain to re-enforce the rules and ensure the children understand the game.

What's in it for the children?
This is a great game for keeping children active. The game really encourages the children to talk to each other, practise turn taking and introduces an element of competition if playing in teams.

Leaf glitter pictures

What you need:
- Dry leaves in various shapes and sizes
- Plastic bag, preferably with a zip lock although this is not essential
- PVA glue

What to do:
1. Collect lots of leaves. They need to be really dry so you might want to leave them somewhere warm for a couple of days.
2. If you are doing this is the autumn, try and get as many different colours as you can.
3. Put the leaves into a plastic bag, squeeze out all of the air, seal and get scrunching.
4. Once the leaves are crushed up you can then use them in the art work.
5. Create a pattern or shape in PVA glue, sprinkle the leaf 'glitter' on the top then gently shake off.

Taking it forward
- You can use leaf glitter as an enhancement to a small individual piece of artwork or you can create much larger scale pieces with a group of children.
- If you have a transient art station outdoors then leaf glitter makes a great addition to children's artwork.

What's in it for the children?
The children will be exploring texture, fine motor dexterity and creativity in their use of the leaf glitter.

Ice sculptures

What you need:
- Lots of large and small containers (plastic or metal)
- Water
- Food colouring or liquid water colour
- Access to a freezer

What to do:
1. Fill all of the containers with water.
2. Add food colouring or liquid water colour and stir.
3. Freeze all of the containers for at least eight hours, preferably overnight.
4. Take the coloured ice blocks out of their plastic containers.
5. Take the coloured ice blocks outside to model with.

Taking it forward
- You could add glitter to the ice blocks before freezing.
- To help the ice blocks to stick together, give the children some water and a paintbrush to use as 'glue'. The ice blocks will freeze the water 'glue' helping them to stick together.

What's in it for the children?
The children will be exploring lots of the skills of building and construction as well as using their creativity and thinking skills.

The children will also have the opportunity to experience the change from liquid to solid and, over time, back to liquid again.

Washing line exhibition

What you need:

- Large pieces of plain paper
- Crayons, coloured pencils or felt tip pen
- Paint (variety of colours)
- Brushes (various sizes)
- Sequins, collage material, glitter
- String or washing line
- Pegs or tape
- Magazine pictures of art work or gallery programmes

What to do:

1. Talk to the children about what an art exhibition is or visit a gallery if you can.
2. Tell the children you are going to hold an outdoor exhibition.
3. Ask the children to work on some pieces of art to exhibit – you can theme the pieces around a topic like 'portraits' or 'animals' or just let the children have free choice.
4. Once the artwork is finished, create hanging space on a washing line outside.
5. You can have one long line or lots of different lines (make sure that there is room to walk in between).
6. Peg up the children's work and admire!

50 fantastic ideas for outside all year round

Taking it forward

- You could invite some guests to view the gallery.
- The children could make invitations and prepare simple snacks.
- Make sure that the height of the washing line is suitable for the audience who are going to view the paintings. You might have to lower it to allow the children to see their work.

What's in it for the children?

The children will be able to apply their creative skills and knowledge to this project. They will also have the pleasure of seeing their work admired on display which is great for their self esteem!

Wonderful waterfalls

What you need:

- Plastic, melamine or enamel plates (various sizes)
- Pots and pans
- Plastic bowls (various sizes)
- Enamel plates (various sizes)
- A variety of baking trays
- Colanders (various sizes)
- Plastic jugs
- Washing-up bowls or buckets
- Water
- Food colouring or liquid water colour
- Spoons

What to do:

1. Get the children to experiment with stacking all of the pots, pans.
2. They need to create a stack that balances.
3. Mix the food colouring or liquid water colour with water and fill up the washing-up bowls or buckets.
4. Put the jugs in the bowls and buckets for pouring.
5. Once the children have got a stable stack, pour coloured water over the top of pans and watch it cascade down.
6. Change the colour of the water with each pour.

Taking it forward

- Experiment with turning the pots, pans and dishes around pouring into rather than onto the colander will give a completely different effect.
- Work collectively to create huge stacks, or join stacks using tubing or guttering.

What's in it for the children?

The children are experimenting with some of the basic skills of construction like stacking and weight distribution as well as experiencing the movement of water over solid objects.

The possibilities are limited only by the children's imaginations!

Make a wind streamer

What you need:

- **Lots of different pieces of fabric** (various colours and textures)
- **Sticks, long and short**
- **Pipe cleaners** (optional)
- **Ribbons in different colours, textures and lengths**
- **Scissors**
- **Jingle bells** (optional)
- **Unwanted T shirts**

What to do:

1. Cut the fabric into strips of various lengths.
2. Tie the strips to one end of the stick.
3. If the children struggle with tying, you can use the pipe cleaners to secure the fabric.
4. Twist the end of the pipe cleaner through the bell and attach to the stick.
5. Let the children run fast to make the fabric flow and the bells jingle!

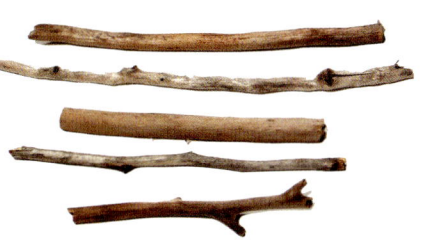

Taking it forward

- You can vary the size of the streamer from small, using twigs, to large using sticks.
- You can push the sticks into the ground outside and let them blow independently in the wind.
- You can give the children fabric pens or crayons and let them decorate plain fabric or old T-shirts before you cut them up to use in their streamers.

What's in it for the children?

The children will be using lots of fine motor physical dexterity to create their sticks and then engaging in some physical activity when they run with them. You can also encourage the children to use their imaginations and turn the sticks into magic wands or magic power sticks.

All in knots!

What you need:
- Group of children
- Space

What to do:
1. Ask the children to stand in a circle facing the middle.
2. Everyone puts their right hand into the circle and takes the hand of someone else. The more random the choice of person, the better.
3. Once everyone is holding right hands, repeat the process with the left hands.
4. The children will now be holding hands with two different people.
5. Now ask the children to untangle themselves slowly without letting go.

Taking it forward
- You could add a time limit for the children to un-knot themselves by.

What's in it for the children?
Apart from using their physical dexterity, the children also have to think and communicate as they will all be moving, stepping and ducking at the same time.